Story by
SIMON FURMAN

Art by
**FEDERICO DALLOCCHIO
BRIAN DENHAM
CARLOS D'ANDA**
and **MIKE S. MILLER**

Colors by
MILEN PARVANOV, CARRIE STRACHAN
and **WILDSTORM FX**

Letters by
SAIDA TEMOFONTE

Cover and original series covers by
FEDERICO DALLOCCHIO
with **MILEN PARVANOV** and **JONNY RENCH**

Variant covers and pinups by
**SHAWN MOLL, SHAWN MOLL & DOUG MAHNKE
SHAWN MOLL & SANDRA HOPE, CARLOS D'ANDA
FEDERICO DALLOCCHIO**

Story consultants:
**CHRIS METZEN, MICKY NEILSON,
ANDY CHAMBERS & JAMES WAUGH**

War Pigs concept by **JASON BISCHOFF**

Special thanks to **KEITH GIFFEN**

For Blizzard Entertainment:

Chris Metzen	Senior VP—Creative Development
Jeff Donais	Director—Creative Development
Micky Neilson	Story Consultation and Development
Glenn Rane	Art Director
Cory Jones	Director—Global Business Development and Licensing
Jason Bischoff	Associate Licensing Manager
Tommy Newcomer	Additional Development
Cameron Dayton	Additional Development

For DC Comics:

Jim Lee	Editorial Director
Hank Kanalz	VP—General Manager
Ben Abernathy	Editor—Original Series
Kristy Quinn	Editor
Ed Roeder	Art Director
Paul Levitz	President & Publisher
Richard Bruning	SVP—Creative Director
Patrick Caldon	EVP—Finance & Operations
Amy Genkins	SVP—Business & Legal Affairs
Gregory Noveck	SVP—Creative Affairs
Steve Rotterdam	SVP—Sales & Marketing
Cheryl Rubin	SVP—Brand Management

STARCRAFT, published by WildStorm Productions, an imprint of DC Comics, 888 Prospect St, Suite 240, La Jolla, CA 92037. Compilation,introductions and pinups Copyright © 2010 Blizzard Entertainment, Inc. All Rights Reserved. Originally published in single magazine form as STARCRAFT #1-7 © 2009-10 Blizzard Entertainment, Inc. All Rights Reserved.

Starcraft and Blizzard Entertainment are registered trademarks of Blizzard Entertainment, Inc. in the US and/or other countries. WildStorm and logo are trademarks of DC Comics. The stories, characters and incidents mentioned in this magazine are entirely fictional. Printed on recyclable paper. Printed by RR Donnelley, Roanoke, VA, USA. 3/10/10.

DC Comics, a Warner Bros. Entertainment Company.

INTRODUCTION

StarCraft.

It is a strange little universe.

Since the original game's launch back in 1998, we've been actively finding ways to continue the stories of the protoss, zerg and terrans—each locked in their seemingly endless war for dominance. Being a huge fan of comics myself, I always figured we'd get around to doing a comic—so long as we found the right creative partners. It took awhile (y'know—ten years or so), but the exceptional team at WildStorm proved to be the perfect match for what we had envisioned.

The book you hold in your hands started taking shape about two years ago. At that point, we were knee-deep in the development of *Starcraft 2: Wings of Liberty*—and still defining the characters and story elements that would form the narrative of that long-awaited sequel. Since there were still some lingering questions as to the fate of our major franchise characters (ie: Jim Raynor, Kerrigan, Zeratul, etc.), we decided to take a different track with the comic series and focus on characters and areas of the universe that would be fun to explore and be a bit less complicated to wrangle (*given the myriad plot complexities on the game-side*).

We realized very quickly that this choice provided us a great opportunity to show our fans the broader scope of the IP, giving them a glimpse at the political machinations at play inside the Dominion, letting them feel the plight of the rugged fringe world colonist, and all around really showcase what life in the Koprulu Sector is like when you're not harvesting crystals or trying to get your firebats to counter a massive zerg rush.

It was Blizzard's own Jason Bischoff who stepped up to the plate and pitched the idea of a group of grim and gritty mercenaries making their way through terran space—one step ahead of the law (*personally, I think Jason watched a little too much* A-Team *as a kid—but then again…is there such a thing as too much* A-Team*?*). Jason and the concept team immediately jumped on this idea and helped to flesh out the broad strokes of the story—and define the various personalities (and fatal hang-ups) of the War Pigs.

Based on the brilliant scripts from Simon Furman (Mister *Transformers* himself) and the gritty, heavy artwork from Federico Dallocchio—the STARCRAFT comic proved to be a fast-paced, hyper-kinetic romp through the seedy, morally-compromised underbelly of the *Starcraft* universe.

Mission accomplished, indeed.

Chris Metzen
SVP, Creative Development
Blizzard Entertainment

INTRODUCTION

"They let you in the door?" (The honest-to-goodness first words spoken to me when I came to interview at Blizzard.)

Tell someone you work in video games and you're the "bee's knees." Follow with the fact that you're the licensing guy, and suddenly you're just another "business jerk."

Don't get me wrong, this strange industry I run around in is full of the above-mentioned stereotype. They can be the worm to the creative apple and sadly, at surface glance, you'd think me one of them. It's typecasting, I assure you, but an easy mistake.

My name's not in the title, nor found on the cover. On occasion (if I'm lucky), check inside, near the legal. I hide there beside: "Associate Licensing Manager." It's a veil, a ruse to lead you off my path. I'm just a business jerk after all, like Bruce Wayne perhaps? Second glances won't be necessary. But don't believe it, don't buy into it for one second. Deep inside this façade lies a furnace burning for the chance to really creatively flex. You, friend, have just thrown a log onto that hungry fire.

Why? Skim the credits again: "War Pigs Concept By." I'm shaking as I type this. I feel the floodgates of chemical emotion swim in my face as I am thankful and unworthy, anxious and shell-shocked. *World of Warcraft®*, *Diablo®* and *StarCraft®* have always been titans of lore to me. How could I have expected to traverse even one of these worlds safely, nonetheless shaped them in some way? How could an "Associate Licensing Manager" have managed court-time with a cabal like Simon Furman, Chris Metzen and *New York Times* Best Selling Graphic Novel author Micky Neilson? (Sorry, Mick, I had to.)

Many years ago, in the primordial days of the mid 2000s, I silently contributed content to some of the biggest brands in pop culture. I cast off those gloves to do what I do now, never thinking that my writing ambitions would be encouraged once again in my new role. Little did I know it would be like being adopted by the family that had wanted me all along. Their patience was saintly. Their welcome astounding. Their opportunity generous. Cheers, guys. Thanks for letting me play.

The broken mess of Terran waste you are about to meet, the WarPigs, were born in seat 31 J (a sixteen-hour prison of my choosing as I flew to Hong Kong in the Spring of '08 for, you guessed it, business). You'll never find the original document that I entitled "Penance Detail" (what was I thinking?), but I can assure you that much of the setup and its stars survived the translation into the ride you're about to take. They were perfected in the weeks to come in Metzen's "Lab." Micky renamed Cole and made Turfa glow (literally). Chris christened the 'Pigs with a name (based off an early SC1 cinematic) and set them off into the fringe worlds on their own ship, the *General Lee*, and Simon—dear "Nemesis Part 2" Simon Furman—made them flipping fantastic.

For the seven issues that comprise this collection (of which I am extremely proud), I've been given a rare taste at what it is that a Senior Vice President of Creative Development does across the hundred-odd feet between our offices. I've got to say it, Mr. Metzen, I'm hooked. Wanna trade for a day…or a lifetime?

Jason Bischoff
Associate Licensing Manager
Blizzard Entertainment

Special thanks to Cory, Hank and James for your enduring wisdom and encouragement!

BEST KIND OF COVER...

HEY, YOU! ORDERLY.

THIS ONE'S GONE. PUT HIM WITH THE OTHERS.

RIGHT.

...FOR THIS KIND OF MURKY, TWILIT WETWORK.

LOOK SHARP, WAR PIGS. MISSION CLOCK IS RUNNING...

BROCK VALEVOSS

ESPECIALLY WHEN THE MAN IN THE CROSSHAIRS...

...IS ARCTURUS MENGSK.

TERRORIST/INSURGENT/ FREEDOM FIGHTER/CHAMPION OF THE DOWNTRODDEN. WHATEVER THE TAG, THE FOUNDING FATHER OF THE SONS OF KORHAL...

...IS CURRENTLY NUMBER ONE WITH A BULLET ON THE CONFEDERACY'S HIT LIST.

STILETTO STRIKE, NO FALLBACK POSITION--THE USUAL RAW DEAL.

THAW *UM*

HUT TT6
MP

BLAM
BLAM

BROCK? BROCK!

NnN-NEGATIVE CONTACT. FFH-CRAP. 'M SEEING DOUBLE, TRIPLE...

TURFA--

--EMERGENCY EXTRACTION!

WHKK--?

NUURA-- GET THE *GENERAL LEE* FIRED UP. SONS SCOPED US TAKIN' POTSHOTS AT THEIR BELOVED GENERAL...

UHT!

TURFA DEI

IGGINS

...AND SUDDENLY WE'RE A DISTINCTLY *ENDANGERED SPECIES.*

ROGER THAT. PICK-UP AND DUST OFF ON YOUR MARK.

WHOA. HOLD YOUR AFTERBURNERS, NUURA--WE'RE JAMMED UP HERE.

S.O.K.?

HOO-WEE! COLE MISSED ONE HELL OF A PARTY. TEACH HIM NOT TO DUCK WHEN THE SHRAP'S FLYIN'.

HAPPENSTANCE, COINCIDENCE OR **ENEMY ACTION?** WAR PIGS ARE EXPENDABLE. S.O.P. AND CORPSES TELL NO STORIES.

ENOUGH ALREADY WITH THAT GUNG-HO CRAP. WHAT ARE WE THINKING HERE?

YAH. AND LET'S FACE IT, THAT ONE DIDN'T EXACTLY GO TO SCRIPT.

NOT THAT WE EVER GET ASKED FOR AN OPINION. OR EVEN HAVE A **CHOICE!**

'TAIN'T THE FIRST TIME WE'VE BEEN HUNG OUT TO DRY. WON'T BE THE LAST.

NUURA?

I WOULDN'T PUT ANYTHING PAST THAT SLIMY CREEP CAULEY. HE'S A POLITICAL ANIMAL, A SURVIVOR.

WHEN JUDGMENT DAY COMES, IT'LL BE HIM AND THE COCKROACHES LEFT STANDING.

HRM. YOU FOUR GO GET **COLE** FROM THAT FRIENDLY E.R. ON RED STONE, THEN GO TO GROUND.

AND **YOU?**

I'M GOING TO KNOCK ON **TAMSEN CAULEY'S** DOOR, LOOK HIM RIGHT IN THE EYE AND **ASK...**

CODED MESSAGE FROM BROCK DROPPED IN ONE OF THE *RIGHT* PLACES.

HE'S CALLING US *IN*.

I *DON'T* LIKE THIS.

NONE OF US DO, COLE. BUT WHAT CHOICE IS THERE?

WE EITHER *MAKE* THE RENDEZVOUS...

AN' EVERYTHIN' ABOUT IT SO FAR CHECKS OUT ACCORDING THE SQUAD PLAYBOOK. NO RED FLAGS.

...OR WE *RUN*. AND *KEEP* RUNNING.

Y-Y-YEAH. IF WE'RE NOT WAR PIGS, WE'RE JUST COMMON "MOST WANTED" SCUMBAGS, AND I FOR ONE AM *NEVER* GOING BACK TO THE HELL-HOLE THEY DUG ME OUTTA!

I HEAR YOU, ROMY, I WAS ON *DEATH ROW*, REMEMBER? IF BROCK IS BEING COERCED, ANY WHICH WAY—

—WE *OWE* IT TO HIM TO TAKE THE HOOK OUT. I'M JUST SAYING...

...WE TAKE *EXTRA* PRECAUTIONS.

I... SEE.

ABOVE ALL ELSE, YOU'RE ADEPT AT READING *BETWEEN* THE LINES.

THERE! THAT IS WHY YOU, TAMSEN-- AS OPPOSED TO SO MANY *OTHER* FORMER CONFEDERATE BUREAUCRATS--FOUND A NICHE IN MY NEW WORLD ORDER.

NEW FOLSOM MAXIMUM SECURITY PENITENTIARY:

LOOSE ENDS, THREADS...

...EVERYTHING THAT COMES OUT OF MENGSK'S MOUTH HAS "COVERING MY ASS" STAMPED IN BIG LETTERS ALL OVER IT. BUT, IN THIS CASE I FIND MYSELF SIMPATICO WITH THE GREAT MAN. AFTER ALL, MAXIMUM DENIABILITY IS WHY I'M HERE, NOW, WITH YOU...

...ONE OF *MY* LOOSE ENDS.

AND YOU **BELIEVE** HIM?

IT'S A BRAVE NEW WORLD, TURFA. CAULEY NO LONGER HAS HIS OWN DEDICATED AND LABYRINTHINE SUPPORT NETWORK.

MUCH AS HE MIGHT NOT LIKE IT, MENGSK HAS HIM ON A PRETTY TIGHT LEASH.

AND THE DEAL IS **WHAT** EXACTLY?

PUT OUR SQUAD BACK TOGETHER FOR ONE LAST MISSION. DO IT RIGHT AND WE'RE FREE MEN. FULL PARDON, BACK PAY, THE LOT.

ONE **BIG** HAPPY FAMILY, EH. REMEMBER WHAT HAPPENED **LAST** TIME?

I KNOW, I KNOW. THERE'S A LOT TO FORGIVE AND FORGET. WHEN CAULEY BROUGHT IT TO ME, MY FIRST REACTION WAS TO TELL HIM TO STUFF IT.

BUT THE ALTERNATIVE IS TO KEEP SCRAPING AROUND FOR PISS-AWFUL JOBS IN THE ASS END OF NOWHERE. I'M **TIRED,** TURFA...

TIRED OF LIVING HALF A LIFE.

I HEAR YOU. SOME MORNINGS I WAKE UP AND FOR MAYBE HALF A MICROSECOND I GET THAT ADRENALINE **HIT**, MY HEART PUMPIN' FIT TO BURST.

BUT IF YOU THINK I'M **EVER** GOING TO TRUST CAULEY AGAIN... YOU'RE SADLY DELUDED. SORRY.

UM. JUST OUTTA CURIOSITY, WHAT'S THE JOB?

STANDARD. LOCATE AND ELIMINATE.

THE MARK?

EX-CONFEDERATE MARSHAL, RENEGADE, AND ALL ROUND THORN IN MENGSK'S BUTT.

JIM RAYNOR.

SHAWN MOLL
DOUG MAHNKE

NICELY DONE, NUURA.

WE WERE LUCKY. THAT'S ALL. AND LUCK IS THE LAST RECOURSE OF THE SOON-TO-BE-DEPARTED. YOUR WORDS, COLE...

HEY...

...WHERE'S THE SLUGGIN' GENERAL LEE?

ᵏDAᴷ DAᴷ

ᵏDAᴷ

VATHUUUMM

C'MON-- C'MON! HAD TO DUST OFF AT THE DOUBLE AND WE CAN'T HANG AROUND.

LISTEN UP...

...WE'LL BE COMING IN TOO FAST FOR BRAKES TO DO MUCH GOOD...

...SO PREPARE TO BAIL.

POOR BABY. SEE WHAT HAPPENS WHEN I LEAVE YOU?

UNIDENTIFIED VEHICLES

IT'S THIS... OR KEEP RUNNING. FOREVER. THE DOMINION'S OFFERING US A FULL PARDON, OUR FREEDOM, *IF* WE TAKE THIS THORN OUT OF MENGSK'S BUTT.

ASSUMING CAULEY HOLDS UP *HIS* END OF THE BARGAIN. LAST TIME, HE USED VALEVOSS TO *RETIRE* US. PERMANENTLY.

THAT WAS *THEN*, TURFA. THINGS ARE DIFFERENT NOW. I REALLY BELIEVE--

WE ARE IN *DEEP* CRAP.

EH? WHAT NOW?

THE *GENERAL LEE'S* VENTING COOLANT. WE TRY WARPING ANYTIME SOON...

...WE'LL BE *SPIT-ROASTED* WAR PIGS!

CAN YOU *FIX* IT?

NOT WITHOUT *EXPERT* HELP. WE NEED OURSELVES A FRIENDLY SHIPYARD AND AN OWNER THAT ASKS NO QUESTIONS.

AND I THINK...

"...I *KNOW* JUST WHERE TO FIND ONE."

GRISSOM IV, APOLLO SHIPYARD:

WE... WE'RE BEING SIGNALED.

ALL THIS TIME, RAYNOR **KNOWS** HOW TO COVER HIS TRACKS.

BEST BET IS TO KEEP SHADOWING THE WAR PIGS. IF ANYONE CAN ROOT RAYNOR OUT... IT'S THEM!

I STILL THINK YOU'RE PUTTING TOO MUCH FAITH IN HICKSON. HE'LL LET YOU DOWN.

HE WON'T. AND IF YOU START **THINKING**, LARS...

...I'LL START REGRETTING MY DECISION NOT TO BRAIN-PAN YOU LIKE THE OTHERS.

CAULEY OUT.

HM.

DOMINION INTERNAL SECURITY DIVISION:

MONICA...

YES, DIRECTOR CAULEY...

GET ME TRAKKEN'S FILE, CHAPTER AND VERSE. I HAVE THE DISTINCT FEELING...

...I'M **MISSING** SOMETHING.

APOLLO SHIPYARD:

RULE OF THUMB IS, IF IT **SEEMS** TOO GOOD TO BE TRUE, IT PROBABLY IS.

THIS ALL A YOU? AH-- WE'LL FIND OUT SOON ENOUGH ANYWAY.

WHELAN, FOOK, JUDGE--SWEEP AND SECURE THE SHIP. ONCE IT'S CLEAR, GET A REPAIR CREW IN THERE--SHARPISH. THE REST A YOU...

...SEE THAT OUR GUESTS ARE SUITABLY ACCOMMODATED.

THE GENERAL LEE.

CLEAR!

CLEAR!

CLEAR!

43

BOTTOM LINE...

...WE WANT YOUR SHIP. *BUT*...

...IT DOESN'T HAVE TO END THERE.

WHO'S "WE"?

THE SCREAMING SKULLS. BUT THAT'S JUST TO SCARE THE TOURISTS. MINUS THE THEATRICS, WE'RE PROFESSIONAL MERCENARIES, SMUGGLERS... WHATEVER PAYS.

AND, DUE TO A RECENT... PERSONNEL CRISIS, WE'RE RECRUITING.

NOT INTERESTED. GIVE US *BACK* OUR SHIP AND YOU CAN *GO* ON YOUR MERRY, MARAUDING WAY. NO HARM...

"...NO FOUL."

HUKK!

WELL, YOU'VE GOT UNTIL WE'RE READY TO LEAVE HERE TO CHANGE YOUR MIND. AFTER THAT...

...DASCH HERE GETS TO PLAY.

44

IT'S DONE.

SO I SEE. SO MUCH FOR THE SCREAMING SKULLS...

...TURFA, WHO YOU GOT DOWN THERE?

THREE MECHANICS, ONE CRANE OPERATOR AND A SUPERVISOR.

FIGURES. CARVER AND HIS BOYS WOULDN'T JUST UP AND KILL EVERYONE. THEY'D NEED AT LEAST *ONE* WORK CREW FIT AND ABLE. TELL THEM...

...THE PRICE OF RESCUE IS A COMPLETE OVERHAUL OF THE *GENERAL LEE'S* WARP ENGINES.

"WHERE NEXT?"

FIGURE WE CAN MAYBE DRAW ON SOME OF *YOUR* OLD CONTACTS, TURFA.

IF MORIA'S ANYTHING TO GO BY, RAYNOR'S BEEN NETWORKING AMONG THE DOMINION'S DISENFRANCHISED AND DISAFFECTED.

IF THAT'S A ROUNDABOUT WAY A SAYIN' I KNOW SOME DESPERATE, DISREPUTABLE TYPES...

THE GENERAL LEE, CROSSING THE KELANIS RIFT:

UH-UH--

--YUHNN... DON'T UNDERSTAND! SHE PUSHED, PUSHED, PUSHED. IN-NN... THE END...HAD TO PUSH BACK.

...HER BLOOD. OH GOD. IT'S... STILL UNDER MY NAILS! I CAN'T... SEEM...TO... GET...IT...

...OUT! HOH-H.

HH-HUUH-HH...

HN.

TURFA, DID YOU--?

WHOLE DAMN SHIP MUSTA HEARD IT! FAT FEST'RIN' CHANCE OF GETTIN' ANY SHUT-EYE WITH IGGINS REPLAYIN' HIS PERSONAL PURGATORY REEL NIGHT-IN-NIGHT-OUT.

WE THERE YET?

NO. AND IF YOU ASK ME AGAIN, TURFA, I SWEAR I WILL PUT A *SPIKE* IN YOUR ASS!

JUST ASKIN'. NO NEED TO BITE MY DAMN HEAD OFF, NUURA.

WELL NEXT TIME, *THINK* BEFORE YOU ASK.

TELL ME SOMETHING...

...IS THIS FOR *MY* BENEFIT OR DO YOU REALLY JUST NOT GET ALONG?

{SNF}

YOU SEE, I'M QUITE CONVINCED OF YOUR COLLECTIVE MEAN AND MOODY DISPOSITION. I REQUIRE NO HARD SELL.

LISTEN, *HOUSTON*, YOU GET TO RIDE ALONG ON THE BASIS OF YOUR GENERAL COMPLIANCE WITH THE "SHUT YOUR FAT MOUTH" RULE...

UF--

TURFA!

...UNLESS, YOU FIGURE ON SHARING YOUR INSIGHTS ON THE WHEREABOUTS OF A CERTAIN JIM RAYNOR!

"...YOU PUT US ON TO HIM IN THE FIRST PLACE!"

HEY.

WH-HUUH!

GOT SOMETHING YOU MIGHT BE INTERESTED IN.

EH? OH. NO THANKS. I DON'T.

NOT STIMS.

SOMETHING MUCH MORE MARKETABLE...

...FOR A MAN WITH THE RIGHT CONNECTIONS.

QUITE THE, AH, TREASURE TROVE.

AND THIS...

...IS THE JEWEL IN THE CROWN!

IS--? IT IS. THAT'S A PROTOSS ARTIFACT, WHERE--?

NO, NEVER MIND. MY BOY...

"...LET'S DO BUSINESS."

YOUR TARGET...

...IS HERE, IN THE MINING TOWN OF *REVELATION.*

MOBILE OPERATION BY THE LOOKS OF IT.

MM. THEY EXTRACT AND PROCESS URANIUM ORE, A VOLUME-INTENSIVE PROCESS. WHEN THE SEAM IS EXHAUSTED, THEY MOVE ON.

IT'S TAKEN ME SOME CONSIDERABLE WHILE AND QUITE A *FEW* FAVORS TO PIN THEM DOWN.

THEY'RE ORGANIZED, USED TO TROUBLE AND CAPABLE OF DEFENDING THEMSELVES.

SO I SEE.

WHAT IS IT YOU WANT US TO RETRIEVE?

MY WIFE. *ELLEN.*

SHE LEFT ME. I WANT HER *BACK.*

THAT'S WHAT YOU MEANT BY YOUR *PROPERTY?* MAN, YOU ARE ONE CLASS ACT, HOUSTON! NO. NO WAY.

I HAVE STANDARDS.

61

HMMGH...

WHAT IN--?

H-HAL? WHAT IS IT? WHO'S THERE?

DAMN!

OHMYGOD!
HELP!
SOMEONE
HELP--

CHUD

M-UT!?

TALK ABOUT A *FIASCO!* WHAT IS THIS ALL OF A SUDDEN? AMATEUR HOUR?

NUURA--

--WE'RE IN. GO-- GO!

"COLE... WE NEED TO *TALK.*"

THIS *AIN'T* WHAT I SIGNED UP FOR!

AS IT IS, WE'RE CHASING DOWN SOME KIND OF FOLK HERO, ON THE SAY-SO OF *TAMSEN CAULEY,* A HALF-MAN, HALF-SNAKE WHO--NOT SO LONG AGO--TRIED TO KILL US *ALL.*

AND NOW, SUDDENLY, WE'RE INTO KIDNAPPING AND COLD-BLOODED EXECUTION.

WE'VE DONE WORSE, FOR LESS.

AT LEAST THIS TIME AROUND IT'S CARROT, NOT STICK. WE GET RAYNOR, THE SLATE'S WIPED CLEAN--WE'RE FREE MEN, NOT EX-CONS ON A DOMINION LEASH. *WORTH* A COMPROMISE OR TWO, I'D SAY.

GEEZ. WHAT A MESS.

HICKSON, GET UP HERE-- NOW!

WHAT? CAN'T IT WAIT, NUURA? WE GOT OURSELVES SOMETHING OF A SITUATION DOWN HERE.

NO...

"...IT CAN'T!"

I'M TELLING YOU... WE'VE BEEN BOARDED.

HOW?

NOT A CLUE. BUT THERE'S SOMEONE OR SOMETHING ON THE CARGO DECK.

RIGHT...

"...WE'RE GOING IN."

73

WE LEAVE YOU WITH A WARNING. THE HUMAN JAMES RAYNOR IS BECOME LIKE A BROTHER TO THE DARK TEMPLAR. SHOULD HE COME TO ANY HARM...

...THERE WILL BE CONSEQUENCES.

HOW'D THEY *DO* THAT? AND HOW'D HE KNOW ABOUT RAYNOR?

THEY READ MINDS. JUST... IMAGINE WHAT IT WAS LIKE TRAWLING THROUGH *OURS*.

I WANT TO KNOW HOW THE DAMN CRYSTAL THING GOT ONBOARD IN THE FIRST PLACE.

THESE, AH, THEY'RE HOUSTON'S THINGS...

...I GUESS *HE* MUST HAVE BROUGHT IT WITH HIM. MAYBE...

...HE HAD A BUYER LINED UP... SOME-WHERE...

LET'S JUST PRAY WE DON'T RUN INTO THEM AGAIN. I GET THE DISTINCT FEELING THOSE THREE PROTOSS...

...COULD HAVE KILLED US *ALL* WITHOUT BREAKING INTO A SWEAT.

SO. WHAT NEXT?

WE START CHECKING OUT INFESTED WORLDS, ONE BY ONE IF NECESSARY, UNTIL WE FIND RAYNOR.

AND ELLEN? WE BLEW *HER* WORLD APART. HER MIND'S JUST *SHUT DOWN*. HOW MANY OTHER LIVES ARE WE PREPARED TO TRAMPLE IN ORDER TO SECURE *OUR* SECOND CHANCE?

RIGHT. WHATEVER WE'VE DONE OR BEEN IN THE PAST, THERE *HAS* TO BE A LINE WE DON'T CROSS. AND RIGHT NOW...

STRAIGHTFORWARD DROP: A CONSIGNMENT OF METAL ROOM-NUMBER PLATES TO CONFUSE THE SPECTRAL SCANNERS, PACKED AROUND A THERMITE DELIVERY SYSTEM.

AND WHAT DO I DO?

I MAKE EYE CONTACT.

BASIC RULE: LOOK BORED. LIKE YOU DO THIS EVERY DAY OF EVERY WEEK AND YOUR MIND'S SOMEWHERE HOT AND TEEMING WITH HALF-NAKED GIRLS. NEVER, EVER...

...CATCH THEIR EYE.

YOU. STEP OVER HERE.

I CONSIDER BRAZENING IT OUT, BUT I KNOW THAT'S THE FAST WAY TO THE FIRING SQUAD...

...SO I CUT MY LOSSES!

H-UUNG!

STAY--

CHUB

THE GENERAL LEE:

...WE KNOW THAT AT SOME POINT, OUR LATE, UNLAMENTED FRIEND *DENNY HOUSTON* HAD A SIT DOWN MEETING WITH RAYNOR.

I'VE CROSS-REFERENCED ALL ZERG-OCCUPIED PLANETS WITH THREE MONTHS' WORTH OF PASSENGER MANIFESTS, LOOKING FOR *ANY* OF HOUSTON'S KNOWN ALIASES AND...

"I GOT TO TAKE CARE OF MY OWN."

HUH?

THAT'S WHAT HE SAID. *TURFA.* TELL ME, COLE...

...WHEN DID WE START PUTTING A SLUG LIKE CAULEY AHEAD OF ONE OF *OUR* OWN?

THANKS TO EITHER THE CONFEDERACY OR THE DOMINION WE GOT LITTLE ENOUGH *ESPRIT DE CORPS* WE CAN CALL OUR OWN. I SAY...

...WE EITHER DO THIS RAT'S-ASS JOB TOGETHER-- ALL *FIVE* OF US--OR NOT AT ALL.

LOOKS LIKE YOU'RE OUTVOTED, COLE. SO UNLESS THERE'S ANYTHING *ELSE* YOU'D LIKE TO GET OFF YOUR CHEST...

...I'M TURNING US AROUND.

COLE?

YOU'RE RIGHT. CAULEY CAN *STUFF* HIS SCHEDULE.

"LET'S GO GET OUR BOY."

AGRIA:

CASTOR MEZZO, SELF-ANNOINTED CHAMPION OF THE KOPRULU SECTOR'S OPPRESSED AND DOWNTRODDEN. WHEN THE CONFEDERACY BECAME THE DOMINION...

...MEZZO NEVER EVEN BROKE STRIDE.

BECAUSE AS LONG AND HARD AS HE USED TO LECTURE ME ABOUT CAUSES AND IDEALS, THE PLAIN, UNVARNISHED TRUTH WAS, FOR MEZZO, THEY WERE JUST WINDOW DRESSING.

FIRST AND FOREMOST, HE WANTED THE ACCLAIM, THE NOTORIETY, AND THE GIRLS AND ROUGH-HEWN GLAMOUR THAT CAME WITH THAT REVOLUTIONARY POSTER-BOY IMAGE.

I WAS HIS APT PUPIL. HE TOOK ME UNDER HIS WING, TAUGHT ME HOW TO FIGHT THE SYSTEM, HOW TO FIGHT DIRTY.

BUT WHEN I STARTED TO SEE THROUGH HIM, STARTED TO EXERCISE MY OWN BRAND OF SELF-SERVING CYNICISM...

...HE DROPPED ME LIKE A HOT COAL, DISOWNED ME.

...JUST ALONG FOR THE RIDE.

MOVE IT. AND KEEP *BEHIND* ME. IT'S NOT MUCH OF AN EDGE, BUT I GOT A... *SENSE*... OF THESE *PSI-BOYS!*

YEAH?

YEAH. RESULT OF AN ABOVE AVERAGE PSI-INDEX OF MY OWN AN' HAVING A TELEPATH BURROWED IN MY HEAD A...WHILE...BACK...

BACK! GET *BACK!* SHE'S HERE!

...ALL SHE HAD TO DO WAS SIT BACK...

THRRTT

DUMB. DENSE. STUPID.

ONCE SHE KNEW I KNEW THE PLACES MEZZO MIGHT'VE HOLED UP IN.

...AND LET ME LEAD HER RIGHT TO HIM.

OH, SH--

THREE DAYS LATER:

IMPRESSIVE.

I'VE SENT WELL OVER A HUNDRED GHOSTS TO DO A HUNDRED DIFFERENT JOBS AND I CAN COUNT THE FAILURES ON THE FINGERS OF ONE HAND.

THE OTHER COLONISTS?

IRRELEVANT.

THE WAR PIGS?

THEY'VE PROVED THEMSELVES QUITE A FORCE TO BE RECKONED WITH. I CAN, AH, *FORESEE* A TIME...

...WHEN THEY'LL PROVE *MOST* USEFUL.

THE ATTACKER IS IDENTIFIED, POST-MORTEM, AS A FORMER INHABITANT OF *KORHAL IV*, STILL NURSING A KING-SIZED GRUDGE AGAINST THE CONFEDERATE POLITICAL MACHINE THAT TURNED HIS WORLD TO ASH.

I SYMPATHIZE.

TO A POINT.

NO, ABSOLUTELY *NOT*. I WILL NOT MAKE ANY STATEMENT TO THE EFFECT THIS WAS SOME *SONS OF KORHAL* ASSASSINATION PLOT. IT WASN'T.

JUST SOME LONE, MISGUIDED INDIVIDUAL WHO HAD LOST EVERYTHING. PRINT *THAT*!

IT HAS TO END.

I CAN'T BE OBJECTIVE. EVERY GUIDING PRINCIPLE I HAVE AND HOLD AS AN OPERATIVE IN THE *SPECIAL SERVICES* IS CURRENTLY BEING COMPROMISED.

NO, I'M SORRY, I CAN'T EXPLAIN. I JUST NEED TO BE REASSIGNED. I...

...CAN NO LONGER GUARANTEE SENATOR CANON'S SAFETY.

AGENT JOSS. I FEEL THIS MATTER IS BEST DISCUSSED IN PERSON, IN PRIVATE. MY OFFICE-- IMMEDIATELY AFTER END OF SHIFT!

I DON'T TH--

THUK

URT!

AGENT JOSS?

I'M ALIVE. AND I KNOW RIGHT AWAY, BEYOND A SHADOW OF A DOUBT...

...THAT'S A BAD THING.

I DO THE WORST THING POSSIBLE...

CARLOS D'ANDA

"NUURA?"

YOU OKAY? HELLO?

HM?

IGGINS. UM. I WAS--

SOMEWHERE ELSE, CLEARLY. OR MAYBE... SOMEWHEN ELSE? ANYTHING YOU WANT TO TALK ABOUT?

TELL ME SOMETHING. IN THE THREE OR SO YEARS WE'VE KNOWN COLE...

...HAVE YOU EVER SEEN HIM THIS... OBSESSIVE...? IT'S BEEN THREE DAYS NOW, AND OF THOSE 72 HOURS I FIGURE HE'S SPENT 64 OF THEM FINE-TUNING THAT DAMN C.M.C.

AND THE OTHER EIGHT GLUED TO THE LONG-RANGE SENSORS.

AS FAR AS I CAN TELL, HE HASN'T SLEPT. AT ALL.

OKAY... THAT IS KIND OF SCARILY NEUROTIC, BUT...

...MAYBE UNDERSTANDABLE. COLE BROUGHT THIS DEAL TO THE TABLE, REMEMBER, PULLED US OUT OF HIDING. SOMETHING GOES WRONG... IT'S DOWN TO HIM.

MM. THERE'S OTHER STUFF TOO. AT FIRST I THOUGHT I WAS IMAGINING IT, BUT THERE HAVE BEEN... LAPSES...

SUCH AS?

FREEZING IN THE SHIPYARD, NO EXIT STRATEGY AT THE VESPENE PLANT, HIS ATTITUDE TO TURFA ON AGRIA. LITTLE THINGS...

...BUT THEY *ADD UP.*

TO WHAT?

PROBABLY NOTHING.

BUT *I'VE* GOT TO KNOW FOR SURE.

"HEADS UP, WAR PIGS-- WE HAVE COMPANY."

THREE SPACE-GOING VESSELS...

...FORMER SONS OF KORHAL STOCK BY THE LOOKS O'THEM.

KEEP IT THAT WAY, NUURA...

HAVE THEY NOTICED US?

UNLIKELY. WE'RE SO POWERED DOWN WE'RE ALL BUT INVISIBLE TO SENSORS.

TRACK ANY INCOMING SHIPS. GIVE IT TWENTY AND THEN TAKE US DOWN.

C'MON, LET'S GET SUITED UP.

MARCUS...

...GOT ANYTHING FOR ME YET?

NOT SO FAR. YOU KNOW HOW TIGHT-LIPPED US SPECIAL SERVICES TYPES ARE.

I'VE BEEN CALLING IN ANY AND ALL FAVORS OWED, BUT SO FAR NOTHING ON YOUR MAN HICKSON. HOWEVER...

...I'VE GOT SOME PULL WITH THE AGENT ASSIGNED TO WATCH OVER CAULEY. CHANCES ARE GOOD SHE'S OVERHEARD SOMETHING.

LISTEN, NUURA...

...WE GO *WAY* BACK. I NEVER BELIEVED YOU HAD ANYTHING TO DO WITH CANON'S DEATH. BUT...

...I'M IN THE MINORITY HERE, AND THEN THERE'S *THE CODE*, BUT...

...WELL, YOU KNOW ALL ABOUT THAT.

YEAH. I KNOW. ORDINARILY, I WOULDN'T ASK YOU TO BREAK THE TRUST, MARCUS, BUT I HAVE A REALLY BAD FEELING...

"...WE'RE *OUT* OF TIME AND OPTIONS."

URONA SIGMA, NORTH-EASTERN LANDMASS:

...SO ACCORDING TO CALLY MULLER, WHO'S PRETTY MUCH TAMSEN CAULEY'S SHADOW AT INTERNAL SECURITY, THERE'S AN EXPERIMENTAL FORM OF RESOC*...

...ONE THAT LURKS IN THE SUBCONSCIOUS AND ONLY GOES FULL BLOWN IN RESPONSE TO A PRE-PROGRAMMED PROMPT.

ANYWAY, THE GUINEA PIG FOR THIS PARTICULAR VARIANT...

*NEURAL RESOCIALIZATION.

...WAS COLE HICKSON!

COLE HICKSON...

...DAMN, IT'S GOOD TO SEE YOU AGAIN AFTER ALL THIS TIME!

HUH?

BUT--

YOU KNOW EACH OTHER?

HELL YES! WE BOTH SPENT SOME TIME IN THE SAME P.O.W. CAMP BACK WHEN I WAS WITH THE 321ST. I OWE COLE MY SANITY. MAYBE MY LIFE!

SO WHEN I HEARD ABOUT HIM AND YOU AND THIS "THING"...

"...I KNEW THERE HAD TO BE MORE TO IT!"

THAT'S WHY HICKSON'S BEEN ACTING SO DAMN WEIRD. CAULEY'S BEEN INSIDE HIS HEAD, TINKERING. IT'S TYRADOR VIII ALL OVER AGAIN!

HE'S GOING TO KILL RAYNOR...

"...AND THE WAR PIGS TOO!"

TURFA? PYRIUS? IGGINS?

DAMMIT, IF ANYONE CAN HEAR THIS, HICKSON'S--

HN.. UP!!

FWHHAM

CAULEY BE DAMNED...

...I WILL HAVE MY POUND OF FLESH, STARTING NOW!

TURAXIS II, 2488:

EVERY DAY THEY KILL ME.

THEN THEY BRING ME BACK.

CAN'T TELL IF IT'S TORTURE OR AN EXPERIMENT.

EITHER WAY...

...IT PUSHES BODY... AND MIND... WAY PAST ANYTHING LIKE NORMAL!

ONLY THE MONOTONOUS REGULARITY OF THE TREATMENT MARKS THE PASSAGE OF TIME.

THE REST IS SENSORY MINIMALISM.

I LEARN TO FILL THE INTERMINABLE GAPS WITH PERFECTLY SCULPTED MEMORIES. INSTANTS REPLAYED WITH HOLOGRAPHIC PRECISION.

ANYTHING THAT DISTURBS THE SIMPLE SANCTITY OF THE REMEMBRANCE...

...I EDIT OUT. OR REWRITE.

INSTEAD OF RUNNING AWAY AT FOURTEEN AND LEAVING MY SISTER TO FEND OFF OUR FATHER'S DRUNKEN ADVANCES ALONE...

...INSTEAD OF LIVING ROUGH AND WEARING OUT SHOE LEATHER UNTIL, IN DESPERATION AND HUNGER, I ENLISTED...

...I EMBARK ON A FREEWHEELING ROAD TRIP WHERE I REACH AND CROSS A DOZEN HORIZONS, ALL PREVIOUSLY, TANTALIZINGLY OUT OF REACH.

I TAKE THESE PROTECTIVE OASES WITH ME...

...INTO THE DARKNESS.

WHERE HORROR AND MADNESS COLLIDE AND COMPETE FOR MY VERY SOUL.

WHERE MONSTERS WE HIDE IN THE DARK CORNERS OF OUR MIND ARE GIVEN FREE REIN!

I FAILED AT JUST ABOUT EVERYTHING. BUT WHEN IT CAME TO WAGING WAR...

...I EXCELLED.

I REMEMBER VIVIDLY MARKING MY FIRST CONFIRMED KILL AND THE MANY THAT FOLLOWED, WEARING EACH WITH A FIERCE PRIDE.

"DAPPER DEATH" THE OTHERS CALLED ME.

I'VE HAD TIME TO REFLECT ON THAT.

TWO WEEKS LATER, BY MY ROUGH ESTIMATION, MY CAPTORS ADOPT A DIFFERENT TACTIC.

I GET SOME COMPANY.

SAYS HIS NAME'S JIM RAYNOR.

THEY KEEP ASKING HIM QUESTIONS ABOUT SOMETHING CALLED RESOCIALIZATION AND STICKING HIM LIKE A PIG WHEN THEY DON'T LIKE THE ANSWERS.

THEN THEY START ASKING ME THE SAME QUESTIONS.

I SUPPOSE THE IDEA IS, WE'RE SUPPOSED TO SHARE.

SO I SAY NOTHING. NOT A WORD. NOT EVEN MY NAME.

IN MY SITUATION, YOU TAKE WHATEVER SMALL VICTORIES YOU CAN GET.

ANYWAY, RAYNOR TALKS ENOUGH FOR THE BOTH OF US.

...SEE, MY DAD, HE DIDN'T EXACTLY TEACH ME RIGHT AND WRONG, MORE WHERE TO DRAW THE LINE. IT WAS A KIND OF *IN-THE-TRENCHES* PHILOSOPHY, ADAPTABLE...

AT FIRST I PHASE HIM OUT, DISLOCATE, TAKING REFUGE IN ONE OF MY MANY MENTAL SPIDER HOLES.

BUT EVENTUALLY, MAYBE BY OSMOSIS, I START TO GET THE SENSE OF A GOOD MAN, A DECENT MAN, KNEE-DEEP IN EVENTS HE'S ONLY NOW BEGINNING TO GRASP.

...SEE THE TRUE SHAPE AND FORM OF THIS CRAPPY LITTLE WAR HE'S JUMPED INTO WITH BOTH WELL-INTENTIONED FEET.

AND FINALLY...

I SEE HIM SLOWLY DISCERN THE LIES HE'S BEEN TOLD...

...I SEE A MAN WORTH *SAVING.*

PLAIN TRUTH IS, THE GUILD WARS ONLY SERVED TO CHISEL THE ROUGH EDGES OFF MY LATENT SOCIOPATHIC TENDENCIES.

BUT IN JAMES RAYNOR I SEE *HOPE*...AND SOME SMALL MEASURE OF PERSONAL SALVATION.

IF I CAN TEACH HIM, SHOW HIM HOW TO RESIST, HOW *NOT* TO LET THEM BREAK HIM...

...MAYBE, JUST MAYBE, I'M NOT A COMPLETELY LOST CAUSE!

DOUG MAHNKE
SANDRA HOPE

WHAT *IS* THIS CRAP ANYWAY, COLE?

WHEN THE DARK TEMPLAR TOLD ME YOU AND YOUR SQUAD WERE GUNNING FOR US RAIDERS, I NEAR RUPTURED MY SPLEEN.

TH' HELL?

COLE?

BACK... *AWAY!*

DAMMIT. THAT FINGER SO MUCH AS TWITCHES WE WILL CUT YOU TO PIECES!

EASY, *EASY.*

COLE, C'MON, WHAT YOU DOIN'? I MEAN, WHY'D YOU EVEN TAKE THIS JOB ON IF TH' MAN'S A BONA FIDE BROTHER-IN-ARMS?

BUT WE *DID* TAKE IT ON.

RIGHT. AN' WE *ALL* GOT A STAKE IN THIS. THE DEAL, MAN, WE DON'T SEE THIS THROUGH, IT'S BLOWN.

WHERE'S THAT *LEAVE* US?

DAMMIT--WHAT IS THIS CRAP? WHY'S HE GONE ALL "ZOMBIE" ON US?

LOOK AT THE EYES. RESOC FOR SURE, MAYBE SOME SNEAKY "SLEEPER" VARIANT THE DOMINION EGGHEADS DREAMED UP.

SKRIJTTCH

WH'T?

HYDRALISK! ZERG'VE FOUND OUR--

CHUP

MOVE! GRAB WHAT YOU CAN AND HEAD FOR THE DROPSHIPS!

EEEIIA!

NOT GOOD ENOUGH. NOT NEARLY. HAVE DELTA UNIT MAINTAIN AERIAL SURVEILLANCE AND--

PROTOSS.

WHAT THE *HELL* DO THEY WANT?

HELM--DISENGAGE DOCKING TUBE AND CUT THE *GENERAL LEE* LOOSE. BRING US ABOUT.

HEADING?

AND GET ME CAULEY AT I.S.D.*...

COMMANDER TRAKKEN, THREE SHIPS JUST WARPED IN.

TERRAN?

IT'S POINTLESS PLAYING CAT AND MOUSE WITH THEM, DAMN MIND-MONKEYS HAVE PROBABLY GOT THEIR MENTAL HOOKS IN US ALREADY. JUST...PUT SOME DISTANCE BETWEEN THEM AND US!

*INTERNAL SECURITY DIVISION

FOURTEEN MINUTES AGO...

≠HUFF≠ OCCURS TO ME WE'VE NOT BEEN FORMALLY INTRODUCED.

JIM RAYNOR, WELL-INTENTIONED MALCONTENT.

TURFA DEI. THIS HERE'S ROMY PYRIUS, AND BRINGING UP THE REAR IS VIN IGGINS.

YO.

AND SOMEWHERE UP THERE, READY TO HAUL OUR ASSES OFF THIS SOON-TO-BE-CINDERED ROCK...*I HOPE*...IS NUURA JOSS.

HEARD YOU MENTION TAMSEN CAULEY'S NAME BACK THERE. HE PUT THIS DEAL TOGETHER?

YEAH. USED HICKSON TO PULL US BACK IN, PROBABLY SO'S HE COULD CLEAN HOUSE.

I DON'T KNOW CAULEY PERSONALLY, BUT I KNOW HIS *TYPE.* DOUBT IT'S AS SINGLE-TRACK AS JUST COVERING HIS OWN ASS.

AND DON'T BE TOO HARD ON COLE. HE PROBABLY DIDN'T HAVE MUCH SAY IN THE MATTER--BEFORE *OR* AFTER!

YOU'RE A BETTER MAN THAN ME, JIM RAYNOR. I WOULDN'T BE SO QUICK TO FORGIVE AND FORGET IF IT'D BEEN *MY* FACE HE STUCK A P-220 IN.

AH, BUT HE DIDN'T PULL THE TRIGGER. AT LEAST, NOT AT FIRST!

DIDN'T...OR COULDN'T?

KNOW WHAT I THINK, TURFA? I THINK COLE HICKSON'S STILL IN THERE SOMEWHERE, FIGHTING.

YEH, YOU WILLIN' T'STAKE YOUR LIFE ON THAT?

I MAY *HAVE* TO.

ZERG! RIGHT ON OUR SIX, *INCOMING!* SWEET MOTHER THEY'RE FAST!

144

BY DAY, I'M A RESPECTABLE MAN-ABOUT-TOWN. AN ENTREPRENEUR. TRUE...

...I DEAL IN HAB, TURK AND OTHER CONTROLLED SUBSTANCES, BUT IT'S GAINFUL ENTERPRISE NONETHELESS.

BY NIGHT...

...IT ALL SHADES A LITTLE DARKER.

THAT ALWAYS BOIL DOWN TO KILLING A LOT OF INCONVENIENT PEOPLE.

IN RETURN FOR THE UNHAMPERED FURTHERANCE OF MY PHARMACEUTICAL ENTERPRISES, I DO THE POWERS-THAT-BE A FEW SUB-RADAR FAVORS.

JOINING ME IN TONIGHT'S LITTLE WETWORK ENSEMBLE ARE...

GREGG MOONSTONE.

KON RENNIE.

BANTA WEST.

JUPITER ROSS.

AND GUSTAV LORCA.

DON'T KNOW ANYTHING MORE ABOUT THEM THAN THAT. DON'T EVEN KNOW IF THOSE ARE REAL OR ASSUMED NAMES. AND MORE TO THE POINT...

...I DON'T WANT TO KNOW.

THE KEY TO THIS ENTIRE ARRANGEMENT IS A LACK OF DOTS TO CONNECT. WE SCREW UP...GET CAUGHT OR KILLED... THERE'S NO WAY TO LINK US DIRECTLY TO THE CONFEDERACY.

I JUST ASSUME THE OTHERS HAVE SIMILAR REASONS TO ME FOR BEING HERE.

DAY. NIGHT. AND NEVER THE TWAIN SHALL MEET.

USUALLY.

THIS TIME I SET UP A LITTLE SIDE DEAL.

I FIGURE TO DO THE OFFICIAL JOB--WHICH IS DELETING A BUNCH OF V.I.P.s, ALL COZIED UP TOGETHER IN THIS HOUSE HERE FOR SOME BIG POW-WOW...

...AND PICK UP A CONSIGNMENT OF BOG.

WITH NEITHER PARTY ANY THE WISER.

RISKY, SURE. BUT THE PROFIT MARGINS ON BOG--SOMETHING OF A RARE COMMODITY ON TARSONIS--MAKE IT WORTH COMPROMISING MY OWN RULES.

IT NEVER EVEN CROSSES MY MIND I MAY HAVE ALSO COMPROMISED THE ENTIRE MISSION...

...UNTIL MUCH TOO LATE.

WARP

I'M INTERROGATED. STRANGELY...

...THEY'RE LESS CONCERNED WITH MY NOCTURNAL ACTIVITIES AND MORE ACTIVELY INTERESTED IN THE NINE-TO-FIVE.

THEY WANT TO KNOW ALL ABOUT MY DISTRIBUTION NETWORK, MY CLIENT BASE. IN PARTICULAR...

THEN I'M GIVEN THE TOUR...

...MY MORE ESTEEMED CUSTOMERS IN THE CONFEDERATE HIERARCHY.

YOU UNDERSTAND ABOUT CUTTING, YES?

THIS IS WHERE WE CUT, BUT NOT TO MAXIMIZE PROFIT. OH, NO.

WE CUT WITH BOURAS, VIVISTYRCHNINE, ZETOX...

I DON'T KNOW ALL THE NAMES, BUT ENOUGH TO GRASP THE INTENT. GENETIC ACCELERANTS, APPETITE SUPPRESSANTS, BIO-MOLECULAR TOXINS, ANTI-COHESIVES...

...A COCKTAIL OF SLOW, DEBILITATING DEATH IN A CANDY SHELL.

WE ARE ALWAYS EXPERIMENTING, LEARNING. NEW VARIATIONS. SO EXTRA RAW MATERIALS...

...ARE ALWAYS WELCOME.

I'M GIVEN A CHOICE: RETURN TO MY OLD LIFE, BE THE MULE FOR THEIR DESIGNER BULLETS, OR END IT HERE, LIKE MOONSTONE AND THE OTHERS.

THEY EXPLAIN THEY'LL BE TARGETING *SPECIFIC* INDIVIDUALS WHOSE DRUG-INDUCED DEATHS WILL INEVITABLY BE COVERED UP BY THE ESTABLISHMENT, LEAVING ME FREE TO PLY MY USUAL TRADE.

IT TURNS OUT THEY KNOW ME...

...BETTER THAN I KNOW MYSELF.

I'M GIVEN ENOUGH OF A WOUND TO MAKE MY ESCAPE FEASIBLE...

...AND SLOWLY THE NIGHTMARE RECEDES. I GET BACK TO MY "NORMAL" LIFE.

WHAT I DID, I RATIONALIZE.

IT'S NOT LIKE WE WERE ANY KIND OF *REAL* UNIT. I BARELY EVEN KNEW THEM.

THEY WERE *ALREADY* DEAD. SACRIFICING MYSELF WOULDN'T HAVE SAVED THEM.

AND SO ON.

NONE OF IT HELPS. THE PAINFUL TRUTH IS I'M A SELF-SERVING BASTARD WHO SOLD OUT HIS ENTIRE SQUAD TO SAVE HIS OWN MISERABLE HIDE. AND WHAT'S WORSE...

OH, HEY, MISTER PYRIUS...

...I'D DO IT AGAIN, IN A SECOND.

...DELIVERY FOR YOU!

SHAWN MOLL
DOUG MAHNKE

THEY'RE VERY... METHODICAL.

MM-HM. I'VE BEEN COUNTIN'. THE INTERVAL BETWEEN EACH BLAST IS *EXACTLY* THE SAME. I'M WILLING TO BET THE SPREAD PATTERN DISTANCES ARE IDENTICAL TOO.

THAT'S THE *PROTOSS* FOR YOU. CLINICAL.

THE SHAME OF IT IS, THEY'VE SKIPPED RIGHT TO THE MASS DESTRUCTION PHASE, NO GROUND TROOPS. MAYBE THEY JUST FIGURED THERE WAS NOTHING HERE WORTH SAVING.

GUESS THEY'RE IN A *HURRY* TODAY.

HEH. YEAH. LUCKY US. IT'S BEEN BRIEF, WAR PIGS...

...BUT FUN.

HAH! YOU ARE SOME PIECE OF WORK, RAYNOR! WE GET ALL BLACK-OPS ON YOUR ASS, COURTESY OF THAT BACKSTABBING BASTARD *TAMSEN CAULEY,* AND ALL YOU CAN SAY IS, *"IT'S BEEN FUN."*

WHAT DO THEY MAKE YOU EX-MARSHALS OUT OF ANYWAY?

SAME AS YOU, TURFA--BALLS, B.O. AND BAD ATTITUDES.

HOW'S *HICKSON* DOIN'?

HARD TO SAY. HE'S ALIVE, FOR WHAT THAT'S WORTH RIGHT NOW, BUT OTHERWISE NON-RESPONSIVE.

IT *COST* HIM T'STARE DOWN THE RESOC* TUCKED AWAY IN HIS HEAD...

...COST HIM DEAR.

*NEURAL RESOCIALIZATION

SCREW CAULEY!

HE MAY BE CONTENT TO SIT BACK AND WATCH THIS PLAY OUT FROM A SAFE DISTANCE, BUT I'M *NOT!*

GET ME A DROPSHIP PREPPED FOR LAUNCH.

I'VE WAITED YEARS FOR THIS OPPORTUNITY. AND NOW IT'S FINALLY COME, I NEED TO SEE HICKSON'S EYES POP AS MY HANDS CLOSE ON HIS NECK, HEAR VERTEBRAE CRACK AS I TWIST.

THE MILITARY SHRINKS WHO POKED AND PRODDED ME AFTER LOS ANDARES HAD A WORD FOR IT...

"...CLOSURE."

169

PROBABLY. THEY KNOW MOST THINGS. MY HUNCH IS THEY *LET* EVENTS ON URONA RUN THEIR COURSE.

THE BOMBARDMENT...

WASN'T EXACTLY METHODICAL AT ALL. THEY'D HAVE *STARTED* WITH THE GREATEST CONCENTRATION OF ZERG, SURELY.

ONLY THEY DIDN'T...BECAUSE THAT'S WHERE YOU WERE! WHERE *WE* WERE.

BUT I THOUGHT PROTOSS DIDN'T DEEM TERRANS WORTHY OF EVEN PASSING CONSIDERATION.

COULD BE...

YOU'RE SAYING THE PROTOSS *KNEW.*

"NOW WHAT?"

CAULEY DID SOMETHING TO MY HEAD AND I'M NOT SURE THERE'S ANY *UNDOING* IT. INDIRECTLY, IT COST ROMY HIS *LIFE.*

SO, WHETHER OR NOT IT'S THE BEST OR WISEST COURSE OF ACTION, NO MATTER HOW ULTIMATELY MEANINGLESS A GESTURE IT MAY TURN OUT TO BE...I INTEND TO RIP CAULEY'S HEART OUT AND *SHOW* IT TO HIM!

IT'S SUICIDE, PLAIN AND SIMPLE.

...THEY'RE IN THE PROCESS OF *MODIFYING* THAT OPINION.

I KNOW. YOU IN?

WE'RE ALL IN.

THE END...?

FEDERICO
DALLOCCHIO

WORLD OF WARCRAFT®

An amnesiac washes up on the shores of Kalimdor, starting the epic quest of the warrior Lo'Gosh, and his unlikely allies Broll Bearmantle and Valeera Sanguinar. Striking uneasy relationships with other races, as well as each other, they must fight both the Alliance and the Horde as they struggle to uncover the secrets of Lo'Gosh's past! Written by Walter Simonson (THE JUDAS COIN, *Thor*) and illustrated by **Ludo Lullabi** (*Lanfeust Quest*) and **Sandra Hope** (JUSTICE LEAGUE OF AMERICA), this is the latest saga set in the **World of Warcraft!**

WORLD OF WARCRAFT
Book Two

Simonson
Buran • Bowden

WORLD OF WARCRAFT
Book Three

Simonson
Simonson • Bowden

WORLD OF WARCRAFT
Book Four (Coming Fall 2010)

Simonson
Simonson • Bowden

WORLD OF WARCRAFT
ASHBRINGER

Neilson • Lullabi
Washington

SEARCH THE **GRAPHIC NOVELS SECTION** OF
WILDSTORM.COM
FOR ART AND INFORMATION ON ALL OF OUR BOOKS!